Foundation Paper 2
Management Account

GW01099350

Second edition January 2003

ISBN 0 7517 0117 3 (Previous ISBN 0 7517 3631 7)

British Library Cataloguing-in-Publication Data

A catalogue record for this book is available from the British Library

Published by

BPP Professional Education, Aldine House, Aldine Place, London W12 8AW

www.bpp.com

Printed in Great Britain by Ashford Colour Press

Welcome to BPP's CIMA **Passcards**.

- They **save you time**. Important topics are summarised for you.

- They incorporate **diagrams** to kick start your memory.

- They follow the overall **structure** of the BPP Study Texts, but BPP's new format CIMA **Passcards** are not just a condensed book. Each card has been separately designed for clear presentation. Topics are self contained and can be grasped visually.

- CIMA **Passcards** are still **just the right size** for pockets, briefcases and bags.

- CIMA **Passcards focus on the exam** you will be facing.

Run through the complete set of **Passcards** as often as you can during your final revision period. The day before the exam, try to go through the **Passcards** again! You will then be well on your way to passing your exams. **Good luck!**

BPP also publishes a Practice and Revision Kit and MCQ cards, which contain lots of questions for you to attempt during your final revision period.

Contents

1: Cost accounting and cost classification

Topic List

Cost centres and cost units

Direct costs and indirect costs

Fixed costs and variable costs

Other cost classifications

Cost codes

Cost accounting is a management information system which analyses past, present and future data to provide the basis for managerial action. Cost accounting establishes the following for processes, departments and products.

- *Budgets*
- *Standard costs*
- *Actual costs*

Cost classification involves arranging costs into groupings of similar items in order to assist stock valuation, profit measurement, planning, decision making and control.

Cost centre

is a collecting place for costs before they are analysed further.

Once costs have been traced to cost centres they can be further analysed in order to establish a cost per cost unit.

Cost unit

is a unit of product or service to which costs can be related.

Example

- Department
- Machine
- Project

Example

- Patient/day (in a hospital)
- Chargeable hour (accounting firm)
- Meal served (in a restaurant)

Direct cost

is a cost that can be **traced in full** to the product, service or department that is being costed.

Direct costs include

- Direct materials
- Direct labour
- Direct expenses
- Total direct costs = prime cost

Indirect cost (overhead)

is a cost that is incurred whilst making a product but which **cannot be traced directly** to the product, service or department.

Indirect costs include

- Indirect materials
- Indirect labour
- Indirect expenses
- Administration overhead
- Selling and distribution overhead

Total product cost

Fixed cost

is a cost which is unaffected by changes in the level of activity.

Fixed costs include

- Rent of a building
- Business rates
- Salary of a director

Costs may also be semi-fixed or semi-variable or mixed costs. For example, an electricity bill has a fixed standing charge and a variable cost per unit of electricity used.

Variable cost

is a cost which tends to vary with the level of activity.

Variable costs include

- Direct materials
- Direct labour
- Sales commission (varies with volume of sales)

Functional costs

are classified as: **production**, administration, **selling** and **distribution**, research and development and financing costs.

Product costs

are costs identified with a finished product and are part of the stock value until they are sold when they become expenses (cost of goods sold).

Period costs

are costs that are deducted as expenses during a period without ever being part of the stock value.

Controllable cost

is a cost which can be influenced by management decisions and actions.

Uncontrollable cost

is any cost that cannot be affected by management within a given time span.

Decision making

Stock valuation and profit measurement

Control

Classify as fixed/variable

Classify as direct/indirect

Classify as controllable/uncontrollable

1: Cost accounting and cost classification

A code is a system of symbols designed to be applied to a classified set of items to give a brief, accurate reference which aids the entry, collection and analysis of those items.

Ideal features of a coding system

- Easy to use
- Unique code for each item
- Easy to expand system
- Flexible codes
- Comprehensive
- Uniform codes

Advantages of a coding system

- A code is usually briefer than a description

- A code is more precise than a description and therefore reduces ambiguity

- Coding facilitates data processing

2: Cost behaviour

Topic List

Levels of activity

Cost behaviour patterns

High-low method

Scattergraph method

Cost behaviour is the way in which costs are affected by changes in the volume of output. Management decisions are often based on the ways in which costs behave. Knowledge of cost behaviour is essential for

- *Budgeting*
- *Decision making*
- *Control accounting*

Costs are influenced by many factors. The most important factor is the level of activity or volume of output.

Level of activity may refer to

- Value of items sold
- Number of items sold
- Number of invoices issued
- Number of units of electricity consumed

Basic principles of cost behaviour

As the level of activity rises, costs will usually rise. It will generally cost more to produce 200 units of output than it will to produce 100 units of output.

In general, level of activity = volume of output

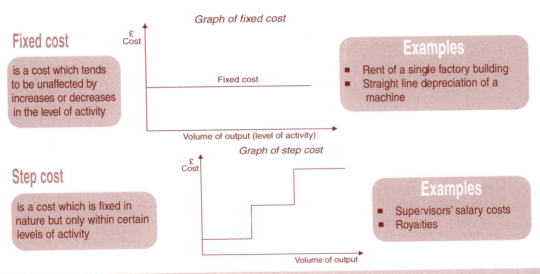

Fixed cost

is a cost which tends to be unaffected by increases or decreases in the level of activity

Graph of fixed cost

£ Cost

Fixed cost

Volume of output (level of activity)

Examples

- Rent of a single factory building
- Straight line depreciation of a machine

Step cost

is a cost which is fixed in nature but only within certain levels of activity

Graph of step cost

£ Cost

Volume of output

Examples

- Supervisors' salary costs
- Royalties

2: Cost behaviour

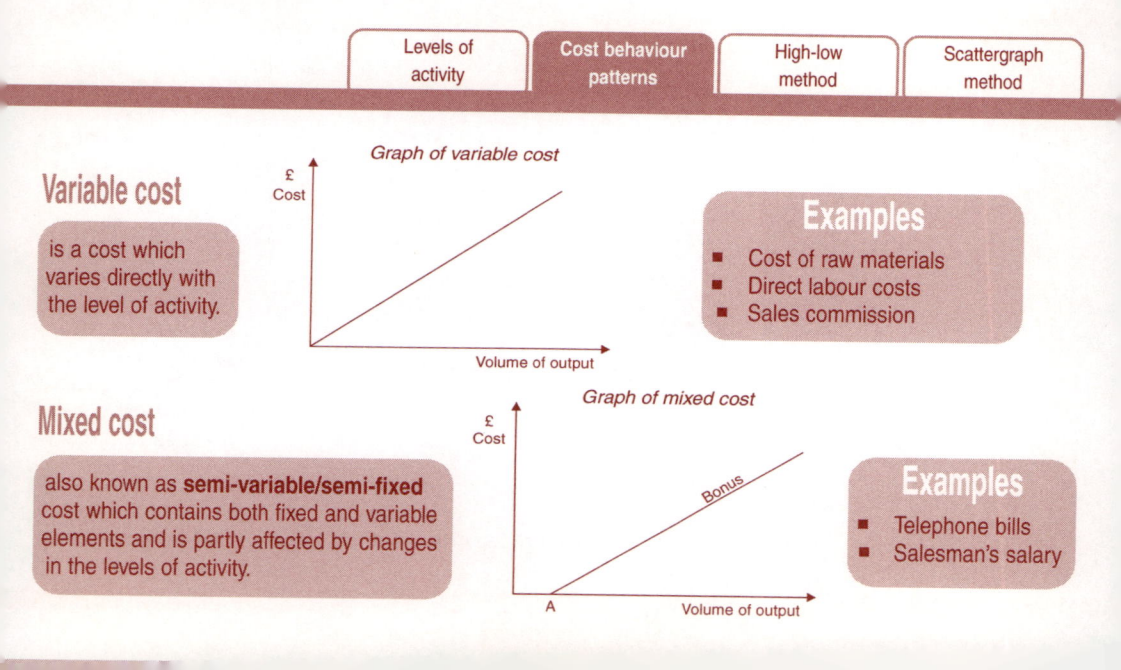

Variable cost

is a cost which varies directly with the level of activity.

Graph of variable cost

£ Cost

Volume of output

Examples

- Cost of raw materials
- Direct labour costs
- Sales commission

Mixed cost

also known as **semi-variable/semi-fixed** cost which contains both fixed and variable elements and is partly affected by changes in the levels of activity.

Graph of mixed cost

£ Cost

Bonus

A

Volume of output

Examples

- Telephone bills
- Salesman's salary

2: Cost behaviour

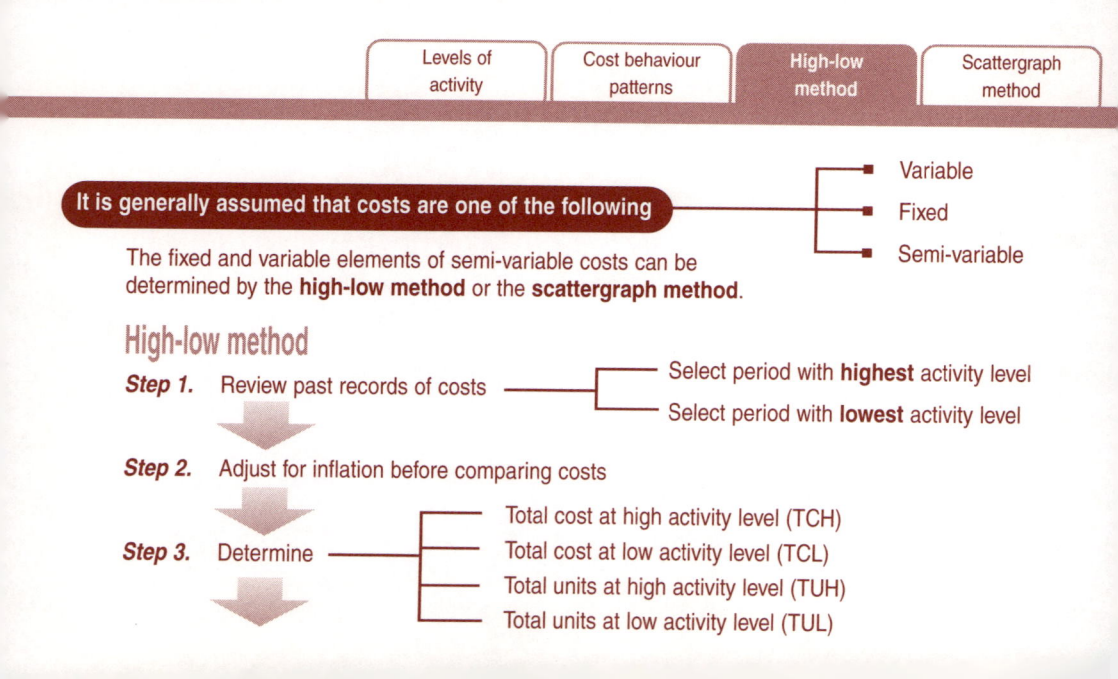

Levels of activity | Cost behaviour patterns | **High-low method** | Scattergraph method

It is generally assumed that costs are one of the following
- Variable
- Fixed
- Semi-variable

The fixed and variable elements of semi-variable costs can be determined by the **high-low method** or the **scattergraph method**.

High-low method

Step 1. Review past records of costs
- Select period with **highest** activity level
- Select period with **lowest** activity level

Step 2. Adjust for inflation before comparing costs

Step 3. Determine
- Total cost at high activity level (TCH)
- Total cost at low activity level (TCL)
- Total units at high activity level (TUH)
- Total units at low activity level (TUL)

Step 4. Calculate variable cost per unit = $\dfrac{\text{TCH} - \text{TCL}}{\text{TUH} - \text{TUL}}$

Step 5. Determine fixed costs by substituting variable cost per unit at high or low activity level

Example

Highest activity level	= 10,000 units at a cost of £4,000
Lowest activity level	= 2,000 units at a cost of £1,600
Variable cost per unit	= $\dfrac{£(4,000 - 1,600)}{10,000 - 2,000}$ = $\dfrac{£2,400}{8,000}$ = £0.30
Fixed cost	= £4,000 − £(10,000 × 0.3) = £1,000

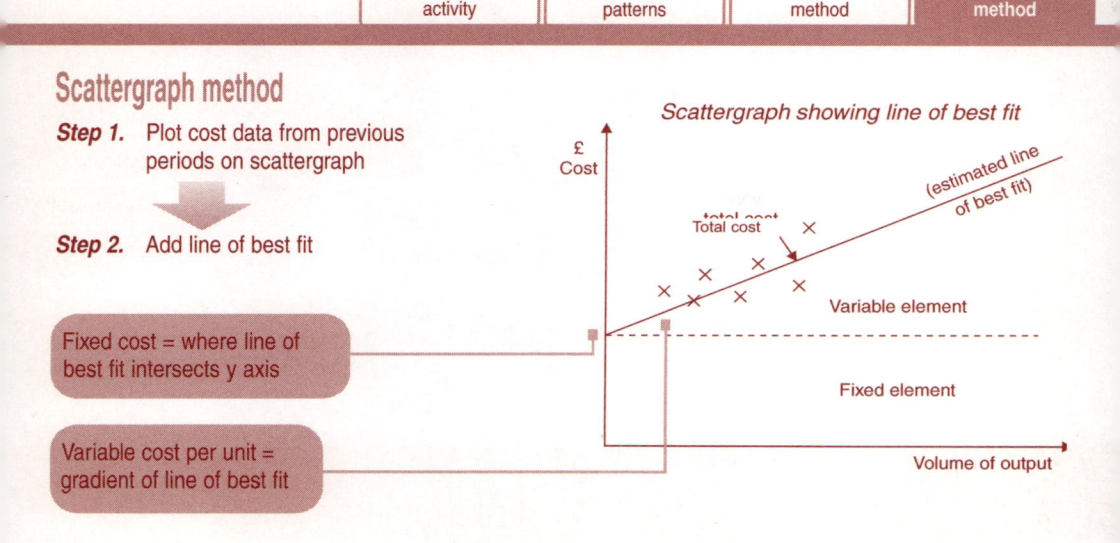

Scattergraph method

Step 1. Plot cost data from previous periods on scattergraph

Step 2. Add line of best fit

Fixed cost = where line of best fit intersects y axis

Variable cost per unit = gradient of line of best fit

Scattergraph showing line of best fit

£ Cost

(estimated line of best fit)

Total cost

Variable element

Fixed element

Volume of output

3: Material costs

*The investment in stock is a very important one for most businesses. It is therefore vital that management establish and maintain an effective **stock control system** which covers the following.*

- *The **ordering** of stock*
- *The purchase of stock*
- *The **receipt** of goods into store*
- *Storage*
- *The **issue** and maintenance of stock at the most appropriate level*

Topic List

Stock control

Stock levels

Stock valuation

ORDERING STOCK

Stock levels reach reorder level

⬇

Stores department issues purchase requisition

⬇

Purchase department draws up a purchase order, copies to

Accounts   Receiving
                  department/stores

RECEIVING STOCK

Goods delivered and delivery note signed

⬇

Delivery checked to purchase order

⬇

Goods received note (GRN) prepared

⬇

GRN sent to accounts and matched with
purchase order

⬇

Invoice checked against PO and GRN

⬇

Supplier paid

Issuing stock

Materials requisition received	→	Stock issued
Stock transferred	→	Materials transfer note
Stock returned to store	→	Materials returned note

Recording stock levels

- Bin cards
- Stores ledger accounts
- Free stock available for future use
- Perpetual inventory

Stock taking

Periodic
- Annually
- All items counted on a specific date

Continuous
- Each item checked at least once a year
- Specialist team

Why hold stock?

- To ensure any unexpected demands can be met
- To meet any future shortages
- Bulk purchasing discounts available
- High stock levels = increased holding costs
- Low stock levels = increased ordering costs
- Low stock levels = increased stock-out costs

Reorder level = maximum usage × maximum lead time

Minimum level = reorder level − (average usage × average lead time)

Maximum level = reorder level + reorder quantity − (min. usage × min. lead time)

Average stock = safety stock + 1/2 reorder quantity

Economic order quantity

is the reorder quantity which minimises the total costs associated with holding and ordering stock.

$$EOQ = \sqrt{\frac{2C_OD}{C_h}}$$

PROVIDED IN EXAM

C_O = Cost of ordering a consignment from a supplier

C_h = Cost of holding one unit of stock for one time period

D = Demand during time period

The EOQ can also be calculated by drawing a graph.

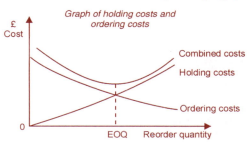

Graph of holding costs and ordering costs

The learning outcomes for Paper 2 require that students are able to explain FIFO, LIFO and weighted average stock valuation methods.

FIFO

assumes that materials are issued out of stock in the order in which they were delivered into stock.

LIFO

assumes that materials are issued out of stock in the reverse order to which they were delivered into stock.

	Receipts		Issues		Balance	
Date	Quantity	Value	Quantity	Value	Quantity	Value
	Units	£	Units	£	Units	£
March 1					10	100
March 10	30	450				
March 12			25			
March 20	20	320				
March 23			15			

Example - FIFO

March 12 issue = $(10 \times £10) + (15 \times £15)=$	£325
March 23 issue = $15 \times £15$	£225
Closing stock = $20 \times £16$	£320
	£870

Example - LIFO

March 12 issue $25 \times £15$	£375
March 23 issue = $15 \times £16$	£240
Closing stock = $(5 \times £16) + (5 \times £15) +$	
$(10 \times £10)$	£255
	£870

Weighted average pricing

calculates a weighted average price by dividing total cost by total number of units in stock. A new average price is calculated when a new receipt of material occurs.

Example

March 12 issue at £(100 + 450)/40	
= £13.75 × 25	£343.75
March 23 issue at	
£((13.75 × 15) + 320)/35	
= £15.04 × 15	£225.60
Closing stock = 20 × £15.04	£300.80
	£870.15

(The 15p is a rounding difference)

FIFO, LIFO and the weighted average stock valuation methods produce different costs of sales and hence profits

Opening stock values and purchase costs are the same for each method

Therefore different costs of sales are due to different closing stock valuations

Profit differences = differences in closing stock valuations

Notes

4: Labour costs

Topic List

Remuneration methods

Labour cost behaviour

Recording labour costs

We have already seen that the investment in stock is a very important one for most businesses. It is also important that the most suitable remuneration policies are employed.

Labour costs is a key area of the syllabus and you can expect to see it tested in the exam you will be facing.

| Remuneration methods | Labour cost behaviour | Recording labour costs |

Time work

- Wages = hours worked × rate per hour
- Overtime premium = extra rate per hour for hours over and above basic
- Quality more important than quantity
- No incentive for employee performance improvement

Piecework schemes

- Wages = units produced × rate per unit
- Guaranteed minimum wage
- Differential schemes pay higher rates for increased levels of productivity
- Output inspected carefully

Bonus/incentive scheme

- Employee paid more for productivity
- Increased profits shared between employer and employee
- High day-rate system
- Bonus schemes (group and individual)
- Profit-sharing schemes
- Incentive schemes involving shares
- Value added incentive schemes

$$\text{Labour turnover rate} = \frac{\text{Replacement}}{\text{Average number employees in period}}$$

Example

The following data relates to Fred's Factory Ltd.

Normal working day	8 hours
Basic rate of pay	£6
Standard time to produce one unit	2 minutes
Premium bonus	75% of time saved at basic rate

Labour cost in a day when 340 units are made = £63

Workings

	Minutes
Standard time for 340 units = 340 × 2 minutes	680
Actual time (8 hours × 60 minutes)	480
	200

	£
Bonus = 75% × 200 minutes × £6 per hour	15
Basic pay = 8 hours × £6	48
Total labour cost	63

Labour costs tend to behave in a step cost fashion. Unless told otherwise, assume labour cost = variable cost.

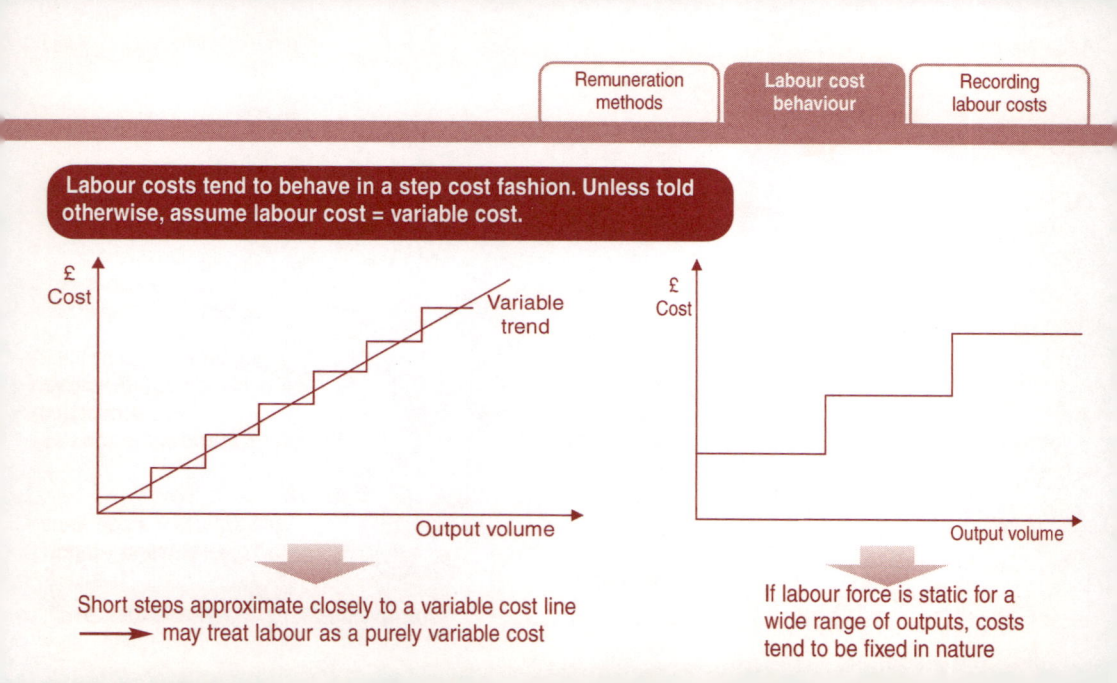

Short steps approximate closely to a variable cost line
→ may treat labour as a purely variable cost

If labour force is static for a wide range of outputs, costs tend to be fixed in nature

Labour-intensive
Direct labour = variable cost

**For control purposes
to measure
efficiency/productivity**
Direct labour = variable cost

**COST ACCOUNTANT
TREATS LABOUR
COSTS AS FIXED
OR VARIABLE**

**Highly automated
industries**
Direct labour = fixed cost

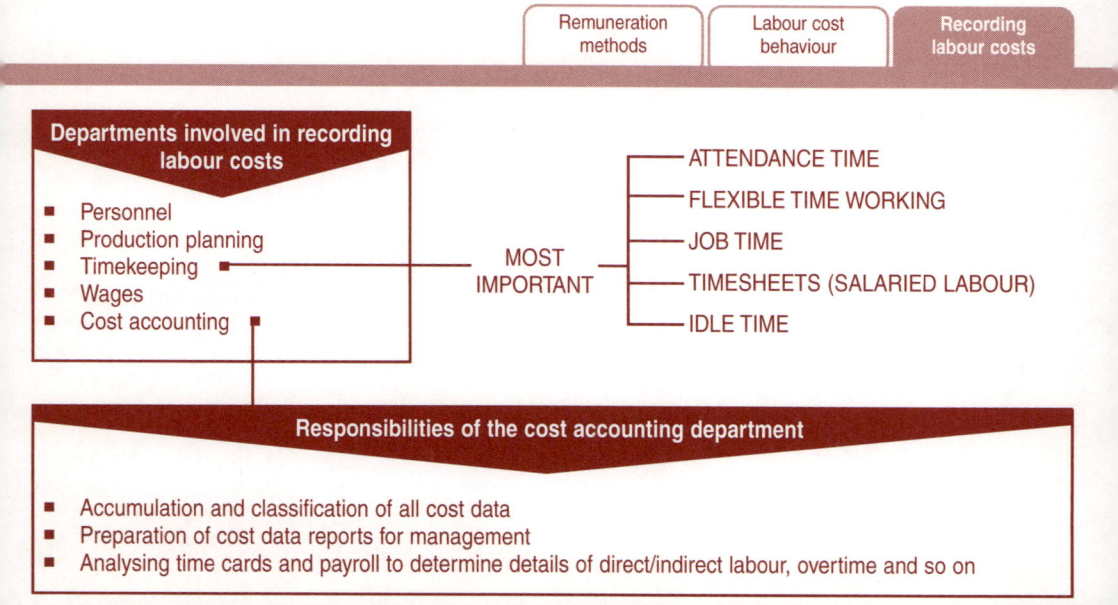

Departments involved in recording labour costs

- Personnel
- Production planning
- Timekeeping
- Wages
- Cost accounting

MOST IMPORTANT

— ATTENDANCE TIME
— FLEXIBLE TIME WORKING
— JOB TIME
— TIMESHEETS (SALARIED LABOUR)
— IDLE TIME

Responsibilities of the cost accounting department

- Accumulation and classification of all cost data
- Preparation of cost data reports for management
- Analysing time cards and payroll to determine details of direct/indirect labour, overtime and so on

Attendance time

- Attendance record
- Signing in book
- Clock card

Job time

- Daily/weekly time sheets
- Jobcards
- Operation card (piecework)
- Time sheets (salaried labour)

Job costing

Idle time

- Occurs when employees cannot get on with their work (through no fault of their own)

- Has a cost because employees will still be paid their basic wage for unproductive hours

- Idle time reports show a summary of hours lost through idle time, and causes of it

- Idle time ratio shows proportion of available hours lost as a result of idle time

$$\text{Idle time ratio} = \frac{\text{Idle hours}}{\text{Total hours}} \times 100\%$$

5: Overhead apportionment and absorption

Topic List

Overhead allocation

Overhead apportionment

Overhead absorption

Absorption costing is a method of accounting for overheads. It is basically a method of sharing out overheads incurred amongst units produced.

The three stages of absorption costing are:

- *Allocation*
- *Apportionment*
- *Absorption*

Allocation is the process by which whole cost items are charged directly to a cost unit or cost centre.

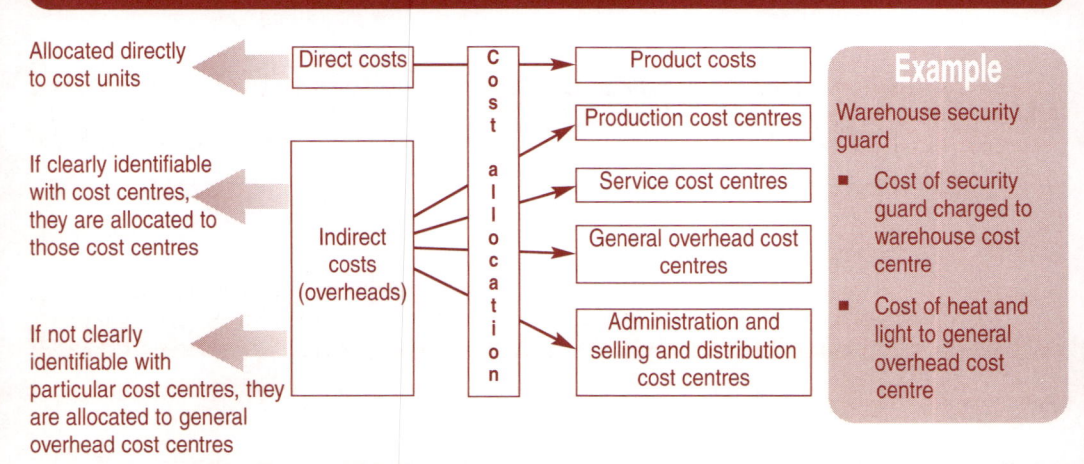

Allocated directly to cost units

Direct costs

Cost allocation

Product costs

Production cost centres

If clearly identifiable with cost centres, they are allocated to those cost centres

Indirect costs (overheads)

Service cost centres

General overhead cost centres

If not clearly identifiable with particular cost centres, they are allocated to general overhead cost centres

Administration and selling and distribution cost centres

Example

Warehouse security guard

- Cost of security guard charged to warehouse cost centre

- Cost of heat and light to general overhead cost centre

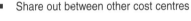

| Overhead allocation | Overhead apportionment | Overhead absorption |

The first stage of overhead apportionment is the identification of all overheads as production, service, administration or selling and distribution.

Overheads within general overhead cost centres
- Share out between other cost centres
- Use a fair basis of apportionment

The second stage of overhead apportionment is to apportion the costs of service cost centres (both directly allocated and apportioned) to production cost centres. This is known as reapportionment.

Direct method

does not take into account the fact that different service departments do work for each other.

Repeated distribution method

takes into account the fact that different service departments do work for each other.

5: Overhead apportionment and absorption

The final stage in absorption costing is the absorption of overheads into product costs using overhead absorption rates (OARs).

Bases of absorption

- Unit (identical units)
- Direct labour hour (labour intensive)
- Machine hour (machine intensive)

Departmental OARs

- Used instead of blanket (single factory) OARs
- Reflect different times spent by different products in production cost centres

Predetermined OARs

Many overheads are not known until the end of a period. If waited until end of period, would cause delays in invoicing, stock valuations and so on. Random fluctuations in overheads would create variable OARs from month to month.

Budgeted overheads allocated and apportioned to production cost centres

Budgeted activity levels (hours, units etc) on which rate to be based

Over-/under-absorbed overheads

These arise because the OAR is predetermined from budget estimates. When actual overheads incurred and overheads absorbed using predetermined OARs, there will be an over or under absorption of overheads.

Reasons
1 Actual OH ≠ budgeted OH
2 Actual activity level ≠ budgeted activity level
3 1 and 2 above (together)

NOPU RULE

NO Actual overhead – Absorbed overhead = NEGATIVE (N) ——→ OVER-ABSORBED (O)

PU Actual overhead – Absorbed overhead = POSITIVE (P) ——→ UNDER-ABSORBED (U)

Remember the NOPU rule in order to determine whether overheads are under- or over-absorbed.

6: Marginal costing and absorption costing

Topic List

Marginal costing principles

Profit reconciliation

MC versus AC

As you now know, absorption costing recognises fixed costs as part of the cost of a unit of output, ie as product costs. Marginal costing on the other hand treats all fixed costs as period costs. Each costing method therefore gives rise to different profit figures which you must be able to reconcile. Similarly, each costing method has its relative advantages and disadvantages.

Marginal cost

is the cost of one unit of product/service which would be avoided if that unit were not produced/provided = variable cost

Contribution

equals (sales revenue – variable (marginal) cost of sales). It is short for contribution towards covering fixed overheads and making a profit.

Marginal costing

- Only variable costs charged as cost of sales
- Closing stocks are valued at marginal cost
- Fixed costs are treated as period costs
- Period costs are charged in full to P&L a/c
- If sales increase by one item, profit will increase by contribution for one item
- Contribution per unit is constant at all levels of output and sales

The difference in reported profits is calculated as the difference between the fixed production overhead included in the opening and closing stock valuations using absorption costing.

MARGINAL COSTING → Closing stocks are valued at marginal production cost

ABSORPTION COSTING → Closing stocks are valued at full production cost

RECONCILIATION

	£
Marginal costing profit	X
Adjust for fixed overheads in stock: + increase / – decrease	X/(X)
Absorption costing profit	X

Stock levels

Increase in a period
- Absorption costing reports higher profit
- Fixed overheads included in closing stock
- Cost of sales decreased
- Hence, profit higher

Decrease in a period
- Absorption costing reports lower profit
- Fixed overheads included in opening stock
- Cost of sales increased
- Hence, profit lower

Arguments in favour of absorption costing

- Fixed production costs are incurred in order to make output and so it is only 'fair' to charge all output with a share of these costs

- Closing stock will be valued in accordance with SSAP 9

- Appraising products in terms of contribution gives no indication of whether fixed costs are being covered

Arguments in favour of marginal costing

- Absorption costing information is irrelevant when making short-run decisions
- It is simple to operate
- There are no arbitrary fixed cost apportionments
- Fixed costs in a period will be the same regardless of the level of output and so it makes sense to charge them in full as a cost of the period
- It is realistic to value closing stock items at the (directly attributable) cost to produce an extra unit
- Under/over absorption is avoided
- Absorption costing gives managers the wrong signals. Goods are produced, not to meet demand, but to absorb allocated overheads. Absorption costing profit may therefore be increased merely by producing an excess of sales. Production in excess of demand in fact increases the overheads (for example warehousing) the organisation must bear

Notes

7: Cost bookkeeping

There are no statutory requirements to keep detailed cost records and some small organisations prepare cost information from traditional financial accounts. Most firms, however, maintain some form of cost accounting system. Cost accounting systems range from simple analysis systems to computer based accounting systems. All systems incorporate a number of common aspects and all records are maintained using the principles of double entry (cost bookkeeping).

Integrated accounts

are a set of accounting records which provide both financial and cost accounts using a common input of data for all accounting purposes.

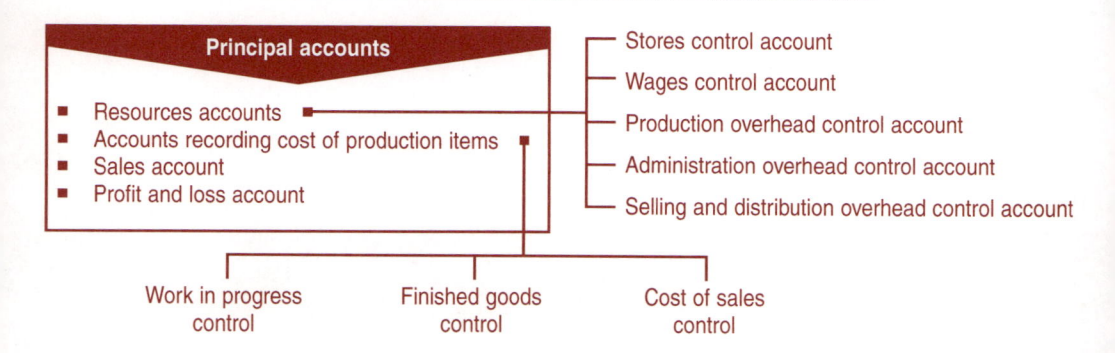

Principal accounts

- Resources accounts
- Accounts recording cost of production items
- Sales account
- Profit and loss account

Stores control account

Wages control account

Production overhead control account

Administration overhead control account

Selling and distribution overhead control account

Work in progress control

Finished goods control

Cost of sales control

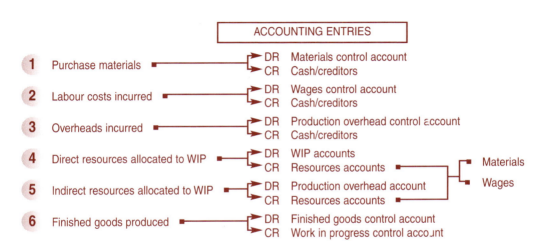

ACCOUNTING ENTRIES

1 Purchase materials
- DR Materials control account
- CR Cash/creditors

2 Labour costs incurred
- DR Wages control account
- CR Cash/creditors

3 Overheads incurred
- DR Production overhead control account
- CR Cash/creditors

4 Direct resources allocated to WIP
- DR WIP accounts
- CR Resources accounts — Materials / Wages

5 Indirect resources allocated to WIP
- DR Production overhead account
- CR Resources accounts

6 Finished goods produced
- DR Finished goods control account
- CR Work in progress control account

7

At the end of a period the following accounts must be completed.

- Cost of sales
- Sales
- Profit and loss

- Administration overhead control
- Selling and distribution overhead control

Balances transferred directly to P&L a/c

COST OF SALES ACCOUNT

DR		CR	
Finished goods a/c	X	Profit & loss a/c	X
	X̄		X̄

SALES ACCOUNT

DR		CR	
Profit & loss a/c	X	Debtors' control a/c	X
	X̄		X̄

PROFIT & LOSS ACCOUNT

DR		CR	
Admin o'head control	X	Sales	X
Selling & distr'n control	X	Over-absorbed overhead	X
Cost of sales	X		
Profit	X		
	X̄		X̄

*Under-absorbed overhead would be a debit in the profit and loss account.

Advantages	Disadvantages
■ Saves administrative effort ■ Less expensive to operate	■ One set of books to fu fil two purposes ■ More detailed analysis of costs required

Wages control account

The wages control account acts as a sort of collecting place for net wages paid and deductions made from gross pay. The gross pay is then analysed between direct and indirect wages.

WAGES CONTROL ACCOUNT

	DR		CR
Bank – net wages	X	WIP – direct labour	X
Deductions		**Production overhead control**	
– PAYE	X	– Indirect labour	X
– Employer's NI	X	– Overtime premium	X
– Employee's NI	X	– Shift allowance	X
		– Sick pay	X
		– Idle time	X
	X̲		X̲

Interlocking accounts

are a system in which the cost accounts are distinct from the financial accounts, the two sets of accounts are kept reconciled by using control accounts or other means.

Limitations

- Profits of separate cost and financial accounts must be reconciled
- Administratively time consuming
- More costly to run

Financial ledger

- Assets
- Liabilities
- Revenues
- Expenses
- Appropriations

TWO SEPARATE LEDGERS

Must be reconciled

COST LEDGER

Cost information analysed in detail

8: Job, batch and contract costing

Topic List

Job and batch costing

Contract costing

Profits and losses on contracts

Job, batch and contract costing are types of costing system. Job costing and batch costing are very similar systems.

Contract costing is different because it involves making a formal contract between the supplier and the customer.

A job

is a cost unit which consists of a single order or contract.

Profit on jobs

Profit may be expressed either as a percentage of job cost (such as 15%) (25/100) mark up or as a percentage of price, such as 20% (25/125) margin.

Batch costing

is very similar to job costing.

$$\text{Cost per unit} = \frac{\text{Total batch cost}}{\text{No. units in batch}}$$

Features of job costing

- Work is undertaken to customers' special requirements
- Each order is of short duration
- Jobs move through operations as a continuously identifiable unit
- Jobs are usually individual and separate records should be maintained

Job costs are collected on a job cost sheet/card

Features of contract costing

- Special type of job costing
- Formal contract between customer and supplier
- Customer has special requirements
- Often covers more than one accounting period
- Large amount of plant used
- *Only* production overheads included in cost of unfinished contract
- Price agreed in advance
- Architects' certificates certify value of work completed
- Customer makes progress payments

Plant hire costs, or if company owns plant, a depreciation charge or a plant account is opened

CONTRACT ACCOUNT

	£		£
Raw materials	X	Written down value of	
Direct labour	X	plant and machinery	X
Cost of plant and		Any unused resources	X
machinery	X	Cost of work done not	
Share of overheads	X	yet certified	X
		Cost of work certified	X
	X		X

Other accounts need to be drawn up.

WORK CERTIFIED ACCOUNT

	£		£
Turnover (P&L)	X	Contractee account	X

CONTRACTEE (CUSTOMER) ACCOUNT

	£		£
Value of work done		Cash	X
(work certified a/c)	X	Balance c/f (debtor)	X
	X		X

The concept of prudence should be applied when estimating the size of the profit on an incomplete contract.

Contract in early stages

No profit taken

Contract 35-85% complete

Profit taken = $\frac{2}{3}$ (or $\frac{3}{4}$) × notional profit
Notional profit = work certified to date – cost of work certified

Contractee withholds a retention/progress payment not made on issue of certificates

Reduce notional profit by the proportion of retentions to the value of work certified.

Profit taken = 2/3 (or 3/4) × notional profit × $\dfrac{\text{Cash received on account}}{\text{Value of work certified}}$

Contract nearing completion

The profit taken may be calculated by one of the following methods.

- Work certified to date – cost of work certified

- $\dfrac{\text{Cost of work done}}{\text{Estimated total cost of contract}} \times \text{estimated total profit}$

- $\dfrac{\text{Value of work certified}}{\text{Contract price}} \times \text{estimated total profit}$

If a loss is expected on a contract, the total expected loss should be taken into account as soon as it is recognised.

Debit contract account with anticipated future loss = Total loss expected – loss to date

Debit P+L a/c with total expected loss = Final cost of contract – full contract price

Example

Contract Zoe is expected to end in 31 March 20X5 and at 31 December 20X4, when the cost of work done on the contract was £157,000, it was estimated that the final cost of the contract would be £193,000. The full contract price is £180,000. Work certified at 31 December 20X4 was £150,000 and progress payments of £140,000 had been paid.

	£
Total estimated loss = £(180,000 − 193,000)=	13,000
Loss to date = £(157,000 − 150,000) =	7,000
Anticipated future loss (taken now)	6,000

Loss is posted £150,000 to turnover and £(157,000 + 6,000) = £163,000 to cost of sales.

9: Process costing

Process costing is a costing method used where it is not possible to identify separate units of production, or jobs, usually because of the continuous nature of the production processes involved. Features of process costing include the following.

- *The output of one process becomes the input of the next*
- *Closing WIP must be valued at the end of the process*
- *There is often a loss in process*
- *There may be by-products and/or joint products*

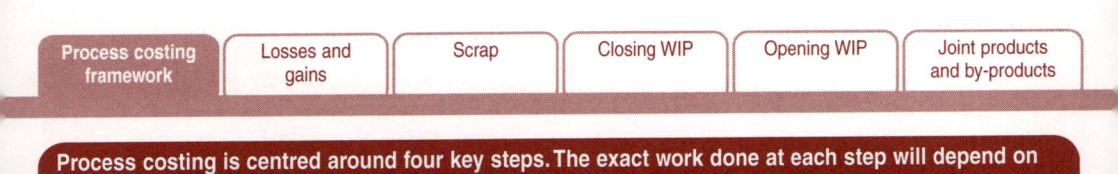

Process costing is centred around four key steps. The exact work done at each step will depend on whether there are normal losses, scrap, opening and closing stock.

Step 1. Determine output and losses
- Determine expected output
- Calculate losses and gains
- Calculate equivalent units if there is WIP

Step 2. Calculate cost per unit of output, losses and WIP
- Calculate cost per unit or cost per equivalent unit

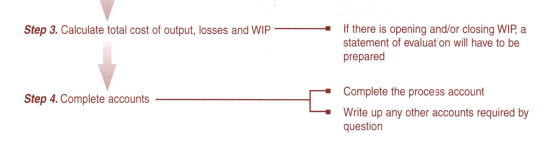

Step 3. Calculate total cost of output, losses and WIP ———— ■ If there is opening and/or closing WIP, a statement of evaluation will have to be prepared

Step 4. Complete accounts ————————————

■ Complete the process account

■ Write up any other accounts required by question

This four-step approach can be applied to any process costing question, so it is a good idea to memorise it. This will save you time in an exam as you won't have to think too long about how to go about answering a process costing question.

Normal loss

is the loss expected during a process. It is not given a cost.

Costs of normal loss are spread across expected units of output.

Cost per unit (normal loss) = £NIL

Abnormal loss

arises when actual loss is greater than expected loss. It is given a cost.

Abnormal gain

arises when actual loss is less than expected loss. It is given a 'negative cost'.

Abnormal losses/gains are taken to the profit and loss account for the period. They are valued at the same cost per unit as good units.

$$\text{Cost per unit} = \frac{\text{£INPUT COSTS}}{\text{EXPECTED OUTPUT}}$$

Example

PROCESS ACCOUNT

	Units	£		Units	£
Costs incurred	1,000	4,500	Normal loss	100	-
			Abnormal loss	50	*250
			Output to finished goods	850	*4,250
	1,000	4,500		1,000	4,500

*Cost per unit = £4,500/(1,000 − 100) = £5

ABNORMAL LOSS ACCOUNT

	Units	£		Units	£
Process account	50	250	P&L account	50	250

An abnormal gain would be a debit to the process account.

Revenue from scrap is treated as a reduction in costs.

REMEMBER! Only the scrap value of normal loss affects the process account.

Normal loss scrap value

- Material costs of process reduced by scrap value of normal loss
- DR Scrap account
- CR Process account

Abnormal loss scrap value

- Cost of abnormal loss is reduced by the scrap value of abnormal loss
- DR Scrap account
- CR Abnormal loss account

Abnormal gain scrap value

- Scrap value is less than expected because there is no normal loss
- DR Abnormal gain account
- CR Scrap account

Cash received from sale of scrap

- Cash received from sale of scrap completes the scrap account
- DR Cash
- CR Scrap account

> **Equivalent units of production provide a basis for apportioning costs between closing WIP and finished goods.**

Step 1. Prepare a statement of equivalent units

Input Units	Output	Total Units	%	Material Units	%	Labour and overhead Units	%
4,000	Completed production	3,200	100	3,200	100	3,200	100
	Closing stock	800	100	800	100	480*	60
4,000		4,000		4,000		3,680	

*800 × 60% = 480

Step 2. Prepare a statement of cost (per equivalent unit)

Input	Cost £	Equivalent units	Cost per unit £
Material	6,000	4,000	1.50
Labour and o/head	4,416	3,680	1.20
	10,416		2.70

Step 3. Prepare a statement of evaluation

	Equiv. units	Cost per equiv. unit	Total value £	Total value £
Completed production	3,200	2.70		8,640
Closing stock: material	800	1.50	1,200	
labour and o/head	480	1.20	576	
				1,776
				10,416

Step 4. Prepare the process account

PROCESS ACCOUNT

	Units	£		Units	£
Material	4,000	6,000	Finished goods	3,200	8,640
Labour and o/head		4,416	Closing stock c/f	800	1,776
	4,000	10,416		4,000	10,416

Closing work in progress and losses

- Prepare a statement of equivalent units

- Deduct the scrap value of normal loss from material costs when calculating the cost per equivalent unit

- Prepare a statement of evaluation (for completely worked units, closing stock and abnormal loss/gain)

- The process account will include normal loss valued at scrap value and values for completely worked units, closing stock and abnormal loss/gain from the statement of evaluation

	Total Units	Material %	Material Units	Labour %	Labour Units
		Equivalent units			
Completed production	X	100	X	100	X
Closing stock	X	80	X	50	X
Normal loss	X	-	-	-	-
Abnormal loss/gain	X/(X)	100	X	100	X
	X		X		X

The average cost method will only be used for process costing and students must be able to calculate normal loss and abnormal loss/gains and deal with opening and closing stocks.

Weighted average cost method

By this method no distinction is made between units of opening stock and new units introduced to the process during the accounting period. The cost of opening stock is added to costs incurred during the period and completed units of opening stock are each given a value of one full equivalent unit of production.

Weighted average cost method

- Statement of equivalent units ────

- Statement of cost per equivalent unit

  $$\frac{\text{Costs b/f in opening stock + costs incurred in period}}{\text{Equivalent units}}$$

  $$= \frac{£(2,800 + 26,400)}{2,940} = £9.932$$

- Statement of evaluation ────

	Units		Equivalent units
Opening stock	500	(100%)	500
Fully worked units	2,200	(100%)	2,200
Finished output	2,700		2,700
Closing stock	300	(80%)	240
	3,000		2,940

	Equivalent units	Valuation £
Output to finished goods	2,700 × £9.932	26,816
Closing stock	240 × £9.932	2,384
		29,200

PROCESS ACCOUNT

	Units	£		Units	£
Opening stock	500	2,800	Finished goods	2,700	26,816
Materials	2,500		Closing stock	300	2,384
Conversion cost		26,400			
	3,000	29,200		3,000	29,200

Joint products

are two or more products produced by the same process and separated in processing, each having a sufficiently high saleable value to merit recognition as a main product.

Features

- Produced in the same process
- Indistinguishable from each other until separation point (split-off point)
- Each has substantial sales value
- May require further processing

Example: oil refining industry joint products

- Diesel fuel
- Petrol
- Paraffin
- Lubricants

Methods of apportioning common costs

1 Physical measurement (eg weight of output)

2 Sales value at split-off point

3 Sales value of end product less further processing costs after split-off point

By product

is a product which is similarly produced at the same time from the same common process as the main product or joint products.

Distinguishing feature = relatively low sales value in comparison to main product

Example = sawdust and bark in the timber industry

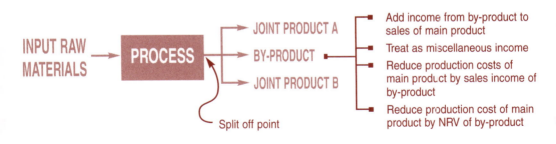

INPUT RAW MATERIALS → PROCESS

JOINT PRODUCT A

BY-PRODUCT

JOINT PRODUCT B

Split off point

- Add income from by-product to sales of main product
- Treat as miscellaneous income
- Reduce production costs of main product by sales income of by-product
- Reduce production cost of main product by NRV of by-product

Notes

10: Service costing

Service costing is a costing method which accounts for services or functions. Examples of service centres or departments include the following.

- *Canteens*
- *Maintenance*
- *Personnel*

Service organisations do not make or sell tangible goods – they provide services. Examples of service organisations include the following.

- *Accounting firms (profit-seeking)*
- *Hospitals (not-for-profit)*
- *Hotels (profit-seeking)*
- *Schools (not-for-profit)*

Two main types of service

- Services provided by a company operating in a service industry

- Services provided by a company's service departments

Characteristics of services

- Intangibility
- Simultaneity
- Perishability
- Heterogeneity

Many services are profit-seeking but others are not. The purpose of service costing might therefore be to provide management information on costs and efficiency rather than to establish profit or loss.

Unit cost measures

Composite cost unit frequently appropriate

Examples

- Canteen - meal served
- Education - full-time student
- Hospital - patient
- Hotel - occupied bed-night
- Transport - tonne kilometre

Cost per service cost unit

$$\frac{\text{Total costs for period}}{\text{Number of service units provided in period}}$$

Organisations need to ascertain the **cost unit** most appropriate to its activities. Organisations within the same industry can make valuable comparisons if they use a common cost unit.

Objectives of service cost analysis

- Compare planned cost with actual cost
- Calculate a cost per unit of service
- Use cost per service unit as part of control function
- Calculate prices for services being sold to third parties
- Analyse costs to assist planning, control and decision making

Internal service situations

- Aim to control costs in service department
- Aim to control costs in the user department

Service industry situations

- Need to calculate a cost per unit as for same reasons as job costs or contract costs are calculated

11: Relevant costing and decision making

Topic List

Relevant costs

Product mix decisions

Qualitative factors

Management at all levels within an organisation take decisions. The overriding requirement of the information that should be supplied by the cost accountant to aid decision making is relevance.

- *A relevant cost is a future cash flow arising as a direct consequence of a decision*

- *All relevant costs are future, incremental cashflows*

Relevant costs

Differential cost

is the difference in the cost of alternatives.

Avoidable costs

the specific costs of an activity or sector of a business which would be avoided if that sector or activity did not exist

Opportunity cost

is the benefit which would have been earned but which has been given up, by choosing one option instead of another.

Relevant cost of materials

- Not owned ──■ current replacement cost
- Owned ── will be replaced
  will not be replaced ──
  ■ higher of current resale value and value if put to an alternative use

Relevant cost of labour

- Direct labour cost plus contribution lost by diverting labour to make another product

  Unless given an indication to the contrary, assume variable costs are relevant costs.

Committed cost

is a cost which has arisen from prior decisions, and which cannot be changed in the short run.

Non-relevant costs

Sunk cost

is a past (historical) cost which is not directly relevant in decision making.

Fixed costs

Unless given an indication to the contrary, assume fixed costs are irrelevant to a decision.

Direct and indirect costs may be relevant or irrelevant depending on the situation.

Example

S plc is bidding for a contract which requires component V (which can be purchased for £170). S plc has a similar component already in stock (at a NBV of £120) which has no foreseeable use. It could however be modified at a cost of £60 and used on the contract.

Relevant cost of component V = £60

The lowest cost option is to modify the similar component in stock, ie £60.

NBV = sunk cost = not relevant

If there is a scarce resource (key or limiting factor), contribution will be maximised by earning the biggest possible contribution per unit of scarce resource.

Assume fixed costs remain unchanged, whatever the product mix

Assume the only relevant costs are variable costs

Example

	T £	J £
Direct labour (£5 per hour)	15	10
Direct materials (£2 per kg)	2	5
Variable overheads	2	2
Fixed overheads	3	3
	22	20
Selling price	£25	£24
Maximum demand	10,000	8,000
Maximum availability of labour	40,000 hours	

Step 1. Confirm limiting factor is not sales

Labour hours required to fulfil demand = $(10,000 \times 3) + (8,000 \times 2) = 46,000$

∴ shortfall = $46,000 - 40,000 = 6,000$ hours

Step 2. Calculate the contribution per unit of scarce resource

	T	J
Unit contribution	£6 (25 – 19)	£7 (24 – 17)
Labour hours per unit	3	2
Contribution per labour hour	£2	£3.50
Rank	2nd	1st

Step 3. Work out budgeted production and sales

Product		Hours		Production	Contribution per unit £	Total contribution
J	$(8,000 \times 2)$	16,000	$(\div 2)$	8,000	7	56,000
T	Balance	24,000	$(\div 3)$	8,000	6	48,000
		40,000				104,000

Qualitative factors in decision making are factors which might influence the eventual decisions but which have not been quantified in terms of relevant income or costs.

Notes

12: Breakeven analysis

Topic List

Terms and formulae

Breakeven chart

Contribution chart

Profit/volume chart

Limitations of breakeven analysis

Breakeven analysis enables management to predict how changes in volume (production output and sales) will impact upon costs and revenues and hence profitability.

Most examination questions on breakeven analysis will require that you can recall the formulae included in this chapter - make sure that you learn them so that you can apply them when you need to.

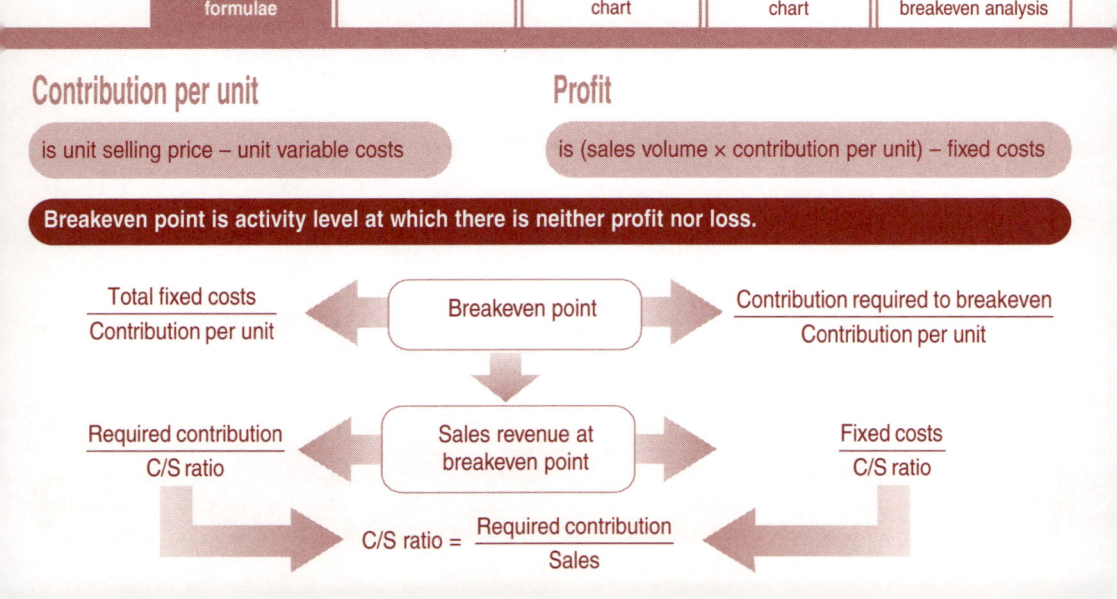

Contribution per unit

is unit selling price – unit variable costs

Profit

is (sales volume × contribution per unit) – fixed costs

Breakeven point is activity level at which there is neither profit nor loss.

$$\frac{\text{Total fixed costs}}{\text{Contribution per unit}} \longleftarrow \boxed{\text{Breakeven point}} \longrightarrow \frac{\text{Contribution required to breakeven}}{\text{Contribution per unit}}$$

$$\frac{\text{Required contribution}}{\text{C/S ratio}} \longleftarrow \boxed{\begin{array}{c}\text{Sales revenue at} \\ \text{breakeven point}\end{array}} \longrightarrow \frac{\text{Fixed costs}}{\text{C/S ratio}}$$

$$\text{C/S ratio} = \frac{\text{Required contribution}}{\text{Sales}}$$

The margin of safety is the difference in units between the budgeted sales volume and the breakeven sales volume and it is sometimes expressed as a percentage of the budgeted sales volume.

The sales volume to achieve a target profit = $\dfrac{\text{Fixed costs + target profit}}{\text{Contribution per unit}}$

- Breakeven point (units) = $\dfrac{£5,400}{£15 - £12}$ = 1,800 units

- C/S ratio = $3/15 \times 100\% = 20\% = 0.2$

- Breakeven point (revenue) = $\dfrac{5,400}{0.2}$ = £27,000

- Sales volume to achieve profit of £3,300 = $\dfrac{£(5,400 + 3,300)}{£3}$ = 2,900 units

- Margin of safety (as a %) = $\dfrac{3,000 - 1,800}{3,000} \times 100\% = 40\%$

Example

Selling price = £15 per unit
Variable cost = £12 per unit
Fixed costs = £5,400 per annum
Budgeted sales pa = 3,000 units

Breakeven chart

Shows the approximate level of profit or loss at different sales volume levels within a limited range.

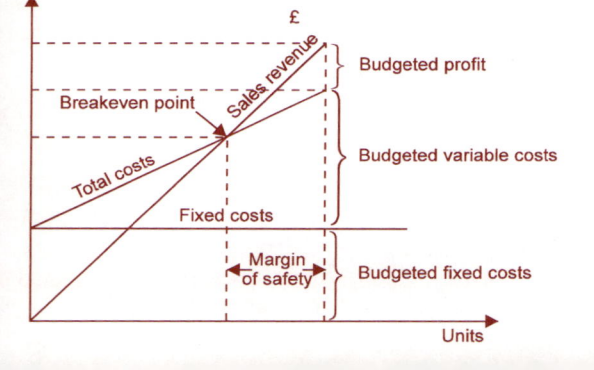

- Profit/loss is the difference between the sales revenue line and the total costs line

- The breakeven point is where the total costs line and the sales revenue line meet

Contribution chart

Draw the variable costs line instead of the fixed costs line on the breakeven chart.

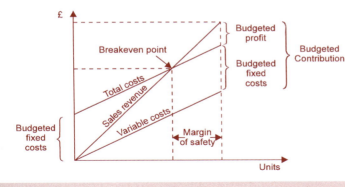

- This type of chart shows clearly the contribution for different levels of production

- At the breakeven point, contribution = fixed costs

- Contribution = Sales revenue line – variable costs line

12: Breakeven analysis

Profit/volume chart

Variation of the breakeven chart. It illustrates the relationship of costs and profit to sales and the margin of safety.

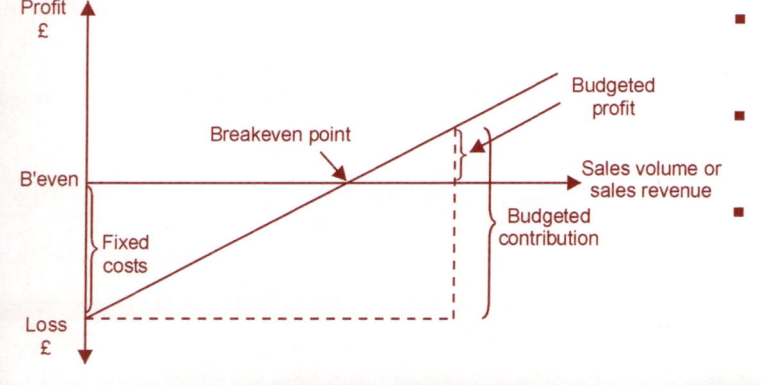

- If the x axis is sales units, the gradient of the straight line is the contribution per unit

- If the x axis is sales value, the gradient of the straight line is the C/S ratio

- This type of chart shows clearly the effect on profit and breakeven point of changes in SP, VC, FC and/or sales demand

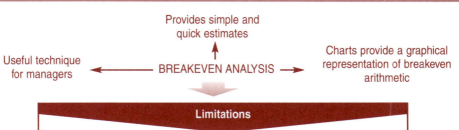

Provides simple and
quick estimates

Useful technique
for managers

← BREAKEVEN ANALYSIS →

Charts provide a graphical
representation of breakeven
arithmetic

Limitations

- It can only apply to a single product/single mix of a group of products
- Breakeven charts can be time-consuming to prepare
- It assumes fixed costs are constant at all activity levels
- It assumes variable costs are same per unit at all activity levels
- It assumes sales prices are constant at all activity levels
- It assumes production and sales are the same (stock levels ignored)
- It ignores uncertainties in fixed costs and variable cost per unit

Notes

13: Preparing the master budget

Topic List

Budget preparation

Functional budgets

Cash budgets and the master budget

A budget is a quantitative statement, for a defined period of time which may include plans for revenues, expenses, assets, liabilities and cashflows. A budget has four main purposes.

- *To coordinate the activities of different departments towards a single plan*
- *To communicate targets to the managers responsible for achieving them*
- *To establish a system of control by comparing budgeted and actual results*
- *To compel planning*

Budget committee functions

- Coordination and allocation of responsibility
- Issuing budget manual
- Timetabling
- Provision of information
- Comparing actual and budgeted results

The responsibility for preparing budgets should lie with the managers who are responsible for implementing them.

- Sales manager → Sales budget
- Purchasing manager → Material purchases budget
- Production manager → Direct production cost budgets

All parts of the organisation should be represented on the budget committee.

Budget manual

is a detailed set of documents providing guidelines and information about the budget process.

CONTAINS

- Explanation of budgetary process objectives
- Organisational structures
- Outline of principal budgets
- Administrative details of budget preparation
- Procedural matters

Steps in the preparation of a budget

Step 1. Identify principal budget factor ———————— ▪ The factor which limits the activities of an organisation

Step 2. Sales budget prepared (units of product **and** sales value), finished goods stock budget

Step 3. Production budget prepared (units)

Step 4. Production resources budgets prepared ————— ▪ Materials usage

Step 5. Raw materials purchases budget (units and value) ▪ Materials stock

▪ Machine usage

Step 6. Overhead budgets prepared ▪ Labour

Step 7. Budgeted P&L and balance sheet

Functional (departmental) budgets include sales budget, production budgets, materials and labour budgets.

Example

XYZ company produces three products X, Y and Z. For the coming accounting period budgets are to be prepared based on the following information.

Budgeted sales
Product X   2,000 at £100 each
Product Y   4,000 at £130 each
Product Z   3,000 at £150 each

Budgeted usage of raw material

	RM11	RM22	RM33
Product X	5	2	-
Product Y	3	2	2
Product Z	2	1	3
Cost per unit	£5	£3	£4

Finished stocks budget

	X	Y	Z
Beginning	500	800	700
End	600	1,000	800

Raw materials stock

	RM11	RM22	RM33
Beginning	21,000	10,000	16,000
End	18,000	9,000	12,000

	X	Y	Z
Expected hours per unit	4	6	8
Expected hourly rate (labour)	£3	£3	£3

(a) **Sales budget**

	X	Y	Z	Total
Sales quantity	2,000	4,000	3,000	
Sales price	£100	£130	£150	
Sales value	£200,000	£520,000	£450,000	£1,170,000

(b) **Production budget**

	X Units	Y Units	Z Units
Sales quantity	2,000	4,000	3,000
Closing stocks	600	1,000	800
	2,600	5,000	3,800
Less opening stocks	500	800	700
Budgeted production	2,100	4,200	3,100

Example (continued)

(c) **Material usage budget**

	Production Units	RM11 Units	RM22 Units	RM33 Units
Product X	2,100	10,500	4,200	-
Product Y	4,200	12,600	8,400	8,400
Product Z	3,100	6,200	3,100	9,300
Budgeted material usage		29,300	15,700	17,700

(d) **Material purchases budget**

	RM11 Units	RM22 Units	RM33 Units
Budgeted material usage	29,300	15,700	17,700
Closing stocks	18,000	9,000	12,000
	47,300	24,700	29,700
Less opening stocks	21,000	10,000	16,000
Budgeted material purchases	26,300	14,700	13,700
Standard cost per unit	£5	£3	£4
Budgeted material purchases	£131,500	£44,100	£54,800

A cash budget is a statement in which estimated future cash receipts and payments are tabulated in such a way as to show the forecast cash balance of a business at defined intervals.

Step 1. Sort out cash receipts from debtors

Step 2. Establish whether any other cash income will be received

Step 3. Sort out cash payments to creditors

Step 4. Establish materials stock changes $\rightarrow$ quantity and cost of materials purchases

Step 5. Establish when creditors will be paid

Step 6. Establish when any other cash payments will be made

Step 7. Bottom of budget must show
- Opening position
- Net cash flow
- Closing position

A CASH BUDGET CAN SHOW FOUR POSITIONS

Short-term surplus

- Pay creditors early → discounts
- Make short-term investments

Long-term deficit

- Raise long-term finance (issue shares)
- Consider shutdowns

Long-term investments

- Make long-term investments
- Expand/diversify
- Replace/update fixed assets

Short-term deficit

- Increase creditors
- Reduce debtors
- Arrange overdraft

PROFORMA CASH BUDGET

	Month 1 £	Month 2 £	Month 3 £
Cash receipts			
Receipts from debtors	X	X	X
Loans etc	X	X	X
	X	X	X
Cash payments			
Payments to creditors	X	X	X
Wages etc	X	X	X
	X	X	X
Opening balance	X	X	X
Net cash flow (receipts - payments)	X	X	X
Closing balance	X	X	X

BUDGETED
BALANCE SHEET

MASTER BUDGET

BUDGETED PROFIT
& LOSS ACCOUNT

14: Further aspects of budgeting

Topic List

Budgetary control

Cost estimation

Computers and budgeting

Learning outcomes for Paper 2 relating to further aspects of budgeting are as follows.

- *Prepare simple reports showing actual and budgeted results*
- *Explain the differences between fixed and flexible budgets*
- *Prepare a fixed and flexible budget*
- *Calculate cost estimation methods using high-low method and line of best fit*
- *Explain the use of IT in the budget process*
- *Calculate expenditure, volume and total budget variances*

Fixed budget

is a budget which is set for a single activity level.

For example, master budgets

Budgetary control

- Establish budgets which identify areas of responsibility for individual managers
- Compare actual results against expected results regularly (using flexible budget)
- Variances are differences between actual and expected results

Flexible budget

is a budget which recognises different cost behaviour patterns and changes as volume of activity changes.

VITAL MANAGEMENT PLANNING AND CONTROL TOOL

Step 1. Decide whether costs are fixed, variable or semi-variable

Step 2. Split semi-variable costs into fixed/variable components

Step 3. Flex the budget to the required activity level

Example

Morgan Ketchgate Ltd has prepared budgeted profit forecasts based on 90%, 100% (50,000 units) and 105% activity. Actual results and budgets are as follows.

	90% £	Budgets 100% £	105% £	Actual (37,500 units sold) £
Revenue	1,350,000	1,500,000	1,575,000	1,075,000
Costs				
Material cost	337,500	375,000	393,750	311,750
Labour cost	405,000	450,000	472,500	351,500
Prod overhead cost	120,000	130,000	135,000	117,500
Administration cost	70,000	70,000	70,000	66,500
	932,500	1,025,000	1,071,250	847,250
Profit	417,500	475,000	503,750	227,750

The flexed budget showing the revenue and costs associated with 37,500 units sold is as follows.

Example (continued)

	Flexed budget £
Revenue	1,125,000 (W1)
Costs	
Material cost	281,250 (W2)
Labour cost	337,500 (W3)
Production overhead cost	105,000 (W4)
Administration cost	70,000 (W5)
	793,750
Profit	331,250

Workings

1 $37,500 \times (1,500,000/50,000)$

2 Material costs are variable, cost per unit = £375,000/50,000
   = £7.50, budget cost allowance = £7.50 × 37,500

3 Labour costs are variable, cost per unit = £450,000/50,000 = £9,
   budget cost allowance = £9 × 37,500

4 Production overhead is a semi-variable cost.
   At 90%, activity level = 50,000 × 0.9 = 45,000 units
   Variable cost of (50,000 − 45,000) units = £(130,000 − 120,000)
   ∴ Variable cost per unit = £10,000/5,000 = £2 per unit
   ∴ Fixed cost = £130,000 − (50,000 × £2) = £30,000
   Budget cost allowance = £(30,000 + (37,500 × 2))

5 Administration costs are a fixed cost

Suppose the fixed budget in the previous example was 100% activity, the budgetary control report would be prepared as follows.

	Fixed budget (a) £	Flexible budget (b) £	Actual results (c) £	Budget variance (c) – (b) £
Revenue	1,500,000	1,125,000	1,075,000	50,000 (A)
Costs				
Material cost	375,000	281,250	311,750	30,500 (A)
Labour cost	450,000	337,500	351,500	14,000 (A)
Production overhead cost	130,000	105,000	117,500	12,500 (A)
Administration cost	70,000	70,000	66,500	3,500 (F)
	1,025,000	793,750	842,250	53,500 (A)
Profit	475,000	331,250	227,750	103,500

Volume variance £143,750 (A)

Expenditure variance £103,500 (A)

Total variance £247,250 (A)

Cost estimation involves the measurement of historical costs to predict future costs.

High/low method

- Graphical method
- Simple but accurate
- Only considers two pairs of cost/output values which are, by definition, extreme

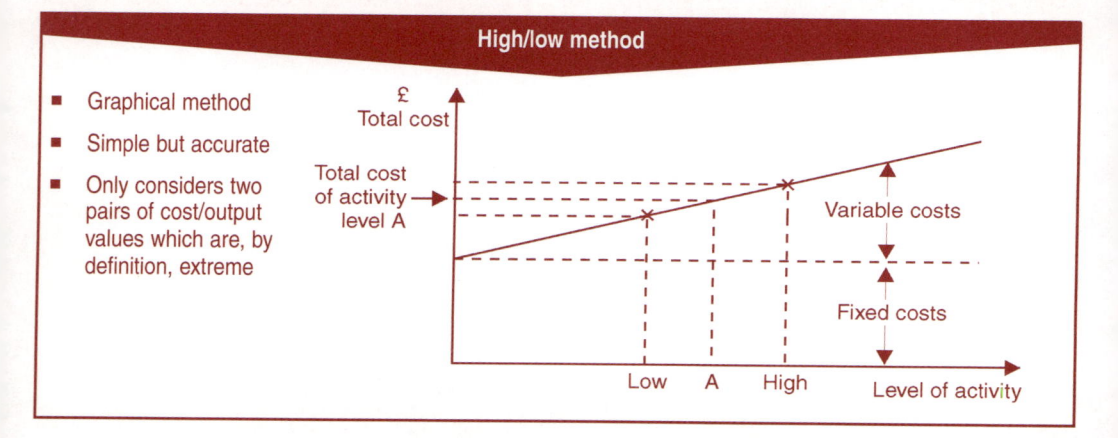

Scattergraph method

- A greater quantity of data is used than in the high/low method but line is drawn by visual judgement

- Plot cost data from previous periods on a scatter diagram

- Add line of best fit

- Fixed cost = point where the line of best fit cuts the vertical axis

- Variable cost per unit = gradient of line of best fit

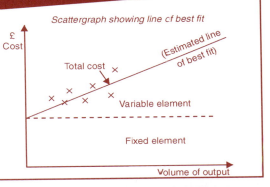

Scattergraph showing line of best fit

Alternative approaches to budgeting

- Incremental budgeting
- Rolling budgets
- ZBB (zero based budgeting)

14: Further aspects of budgeting

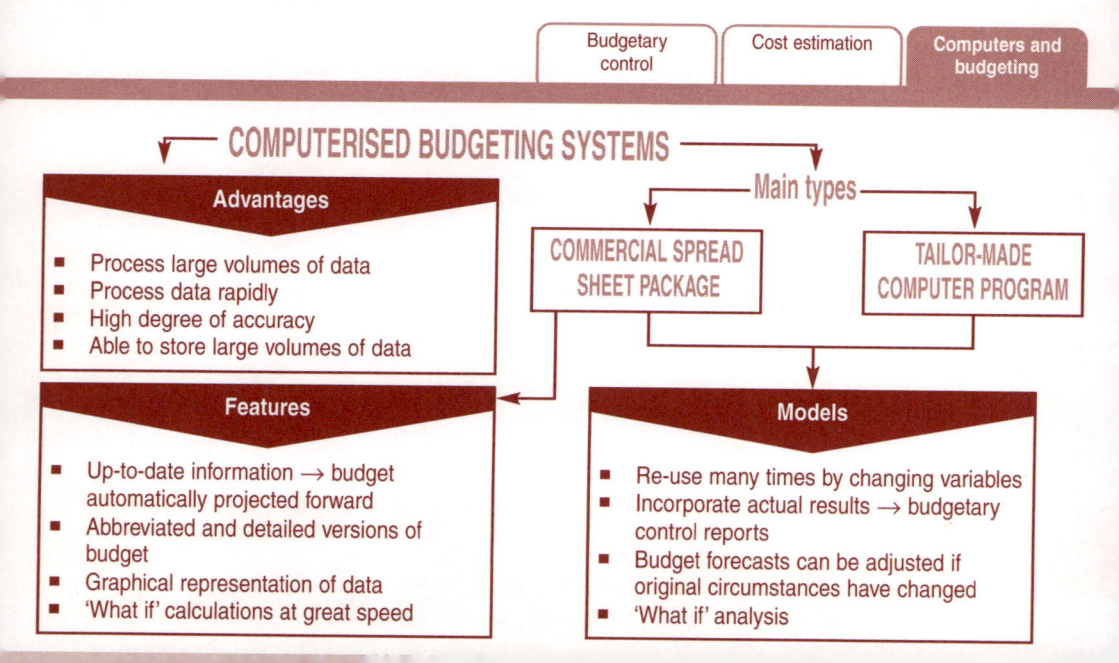

COMPUTERISED BUDGETING SYSTEMS

Advantages

- Process large volumes of data
- Process data rapidly
- High degree of accuracy
- Able to store large volumes of data

Main types

COMMERCIAL SPREAD SHEET PACKAGE

TAILOR-MADE COMPUTER PROGRAM

Features

- Up-to-date information → budget automatically projected forward
- Abbreviated and detailed versions of budget
- Graphical representation of data
- 'What if' calculations at great speed

Models

- Re-use many times by changing variables
- Incorporate actual results → budgetary control reports
- Budget forecasts can be adjusted if original circumstances have changed
- 'What if' analysis

15: Introduction to standard costing

A standard cost is an estimated unit cost built up from standards for each cost element. It is based on estimates of the following.

- *Expected prices of materials, labour and expenses*
- *Efficiency levels in the use of materials and labour*
- *Budgeted overhead costs and budgeted levels of activity*

Standard costing

is a control technique which compares standard costs and revenues with actual results to obtain variances which are used to stimulate improved performance.

The total standard cost of a product is built up from standards for each cost element

USES

- To value stocks and cost production
- To act as a control device via variance analysis

Examples

- Standard quantities of materials at standard prices

- Standard quantities of labour time at standard rates

STANDARD COST CARD

PRODUCT LW

	£
Direct material (standard quantity × standard price)	X
Direct labour (standard time × standard rate)	X
Standard direct cost	X
Variable production overhead (standard time × standard rate)	X
Standard variable cost of production	X
Fixed production overhead (standard time × standard rate)	X
Standard full production cost	X
Administration and marketing overhead	X
Standard cost of sale	X
Standard profit	X
Standard selling price	X

Material price standards

- Estimated by purchasing department
- Problems of allowing for inflation

Labour rate standards

- Set by reference to payroll records
- Average rate for each grade of employee
- Problem of wage rate inflation

Overheads

- Standard absorption rate = predetermined rate OAR

$$OAR = \frac{Budgeted\ overheads}{Budgeted\ activity\ level}$$

Material usage and labour efficiency

Technical specifications
- Standard product specification
- Standard operation sheet

Types of standard
- Ideal
- Attainable

Problems
- Inflation
- Choice of an efficiency standard
- Materials quality versus wastage
- Accounting for price variations/discounts
- Behavioural problems
- Cost of setting up
- Time to set up

The standard hour is a useful measure that can be used to monitor output in a standard costing system. It overcomes the problem of measuring output when a number of dissimilar products are manufactured.

Standard hour

is the quantity of work achievable at standard performance, expressed in terms of a standard unit of work done in a standard period of time.

Example

Golf Ltd manufactures cups, saucers and teapots.

	Production		Standard	Standard hours	
	Year 1	Year 2	time	Year 1	Year 2
Cups	1,000	800	1/2 hour	500	400
Saucers	1,200	1,500	1/3 hour	400	500
Teapots	800	900	1/4 hour	200	225
				1,100	1,125

The output level in the two years was therefore very similar.

Criticisms of standard costing

- Control and operations not always repetitive → standard costing relies on this

- Standard costing systems developed when business environment stable and unchanging → cannot assume stability in current environment

- Current business environment focused on continuous improvement → standard costing assumes standard performance acceptable

- Standard costing developed when mass/repetitive production predominant → current environment sees growth in service sector

Adaptations

- Some standard components may be identified even when output not standard

- Computers enable standards to be updated rapidly and frequently → remain useful for control

- Use of ideal standards and more demanding performance levels → continuous improvement

- Can be applied in service industries where a measureable cost unit can be established

16: Basic variance analysis

A variance is the difference between an actual result and an expected result.

Variance analysis is the process by which the total difference between standards and actual results is analysed. When actual results are better than expected results, we have a favourable variance (F). When actual results are worse than expected results we have an adverse (A) variance.

Direct material total variance

	£
1,000 units should have cost	100,000
but did cost	98,600
Direct material total variance	1,400 (F)

Example

Product LW has a standard direct material cost as follows.

10 kg of material M at £10 per kg = £100 per unit of M.

During a period, 1,000 units of LW were manufactured, using 11,700 kg of material M, which cost £98,600.

Direct material price

	£
11,700 kg of M should have cost	117,000
but did cost	98,600
Material M price variance	18,400 (F)

Direct material usage

1,000 units should have used (× 10 kg)	10,000 kg
but did use	11,700 kg
Usage variance in kgs	1,700 kg (A)
× standard cost per kilogram	× £10
Material M usage variance	£17,000 (A)

Direct material cost variance = material price variance + material usage variance

Direct labour total variance

	£
1,500 units of product LW	
should have cost (× £10)	15,000
but did cost	17,500
Direct labour total variance	2,500 (A)

Direct labour rate variance

	£
3,080 hours of grade A labour	
should have cost (× £5)	15,400
but did cost	17,500
Direct labour rate variance	2,100 (A)

Idle time variance = idle hours × standard rate per hour = 100 × £5 = £500 (A)

Example

The standard direct labour cost of product LW is as follows.

2 hours of grade A labour at £5 per hour = £10 per unit of product LW

During a period, 1,500 units of product LW were made, and the direct labour cost of grade A labour was £17,500 for 3,080 hours of work. 100 hours were recorded as idle time.

Direct labour efficiency variance

1,500 units of product LW	
should take (× 2 hours)	3,000 hrs
but did take (3,080 – 100)	2,980 hrs
Direct labour efficiency variance in hrs	20 hrs (F)
× standard rate per hour	× £5
Direct labour efficiency variance in £	100 (F)

Direct labour total variance = labour rate variance + labour efficiency variance

16: Basic variance analysis

Example

The variable production overhead cost of product LW is as follows.

2 hours @ £1.50 = £3 per unit

During a period, 6,400 units of product LW were made. The labour force worked 820 hours, of which 60 were recorded as idle time. The variable overhead cost was £1,230.

Expenditure variance

	£
760 hours of var. prod. o'head should cost (× £1.50)	1,140
but did cost	1,230
Variable production overhead expenditure variance	90 (A)

Efficiency variance

400 units of product LW should take (× 2 hrs)	800 hrs
but did take (active)	760 hrs
Variable prod. o'head efficiency variance in hours	40 hrs (F)
× standard rate per hour	× £1.50
Variable production overhead efficiency variance in £	£60 (F)

In an absorption costing system, fixed production overhead variances are an attempt to explain the under or over absorption of fixed production overheads.

Method of calculating cost variances for variable cost items is essentially same for materials, labour and overheads.

Calculation of fixed production overheads is very different **FIXED PRODUCTION OVERHEAD TOTAL VARIANCE** **EXPENDITURE VARIANCE**

VOLUME VARIANCE

Remember that in standard absorption costing systems where dissimilar units are manufactured, fixed production overheads are absorbed using a predetermined rate per standard hour (machine or labour). The fixed production overhead variances in standard absorption costing systems are calculated in the usual way but use standard hours instead of units.

16: Basic variance analysis

Example

Budgeted production 1,000 units of product A

Actual fixed overhead expenditure = £20,450

Time required to produce one unit of product A = 5 hours

Actual production = 1,100 units of A

Budgeted fixed overhead = £20,000

Actual hours worked = £5,400

Standard fixed overhead cost per unit of product A = £20 per unit

	£
Fixed overhead incurred	20,450
Fixed overhead absorbed (1,100 × £20)	22,000
Fixed overhead total variance	1,550 (F)

■ over-absorbed overhead

Adverse variance because actual expenditure was greater than budgeted expenditure

	£
Budgeted fixed overhead expenditure	20,000
Actual fixed overhead expenditure	20,450
Fixed overhead expenditure variance	450 (A) ■

	£
Actual production at std rate (1,100 × £20)	22,000
Budgeted production at std rate (1,000 × £20)	20,000
Fixed overhead volume variance	2,000 (F) ■

Favourable variance because output was greater than expected

Material price

Favourable	Adverse
Unforeseen discounts	Price increase
Material std changed	Careless purchasing

Material usage

Favourable	Adverse
Higher quality material	Defective material
Effective use of material	Excessive waste

Variable and fixed overhead

Favourable	Adverse
Cost savings	Excessive use

Labour rate

Favourable	Adverse
Lower rate paid	Wage rate increase

Idle time

Machine breakdown
Illness/injury

Labour efficiency

Favourable	Adverse
Motivated staff	Lack of training
Quality materials	Sub-std material

Interdependence

The cause of one variance (adverse) might be wholly or partly explained by the cause of another favourable variance.

- Material price and usage variances

- Material price and labour efficiency variances

- Labour rate and efficiency variances

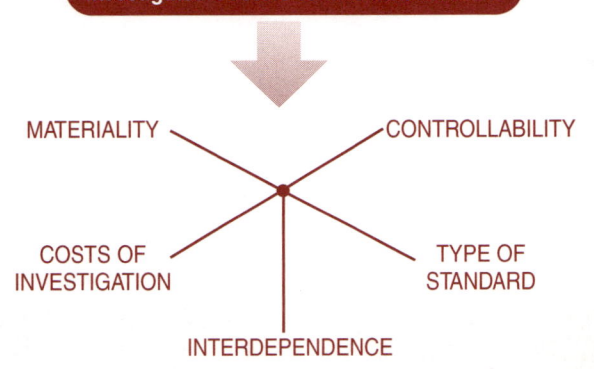

Significant variances should be investigated. Factors to take into account:

MATERIALITY

CONTROLLABILITY

COSTS OF INVESTIGATION

TYPE OF STANDARD

INTERDEPENDENCE

17: Further variance analysis

The objective of cost variance analysis is to assist management in the control of costs. Costs are, however, only one of the factors which contribute to the achievement of planned profit. Sales are another important factor and the total sales margin variance can be calculated to aid management's control of their business.

Variances can be presented to management in operating statements.

Selling price variance

is a measure of the effect on expected profit of a different selling price to standard selling price.

Example

The standard selling price of product H is £15. Actual sales in 2001 were 2,000 units at £15.30 per unit. Budgeted sales were 2,200 units and standard full cost per unit of H is £12.30.

Sales volume profit variance

is the difference between actual units sold and the budgeted quantity, valued at the standard profit per unit.

Selling price variance

	£
Sales revenue from 2,000 units	
should have been (× £15)	30,000
but was (× £15.30)	30,600
Selling price variance	600 (F) ▪

Favourable variance because the price was higher than expected

Sales volume profit variance

Budgeted sales volume	2,200
Actual sales volume	2,000
	200 (A)
× standard profit per unit (£15.30 − £12.30)	× £3
Sales volume profit variance	600 (A) ▪

Adverse variance because actual sales were less than budgeted

OPERATING STATEMENT

> An operating statement is a regular report for management of actual cost and revenues, as appropriate. It will usually compare actual with budget to show variances.

	£	£
Budgeted profit before sales and administration costs		X
Total sales margin variance		X
Actual sales minus standard cost of sales		X

Cost variances	£	£	£
	(F)	(A)	
Material price	X		
Material usage etc		X	
	X	X	
Sales and administration costs			X
Actual profit			X

17: Further variance analysis

If an organisation uses standard marginal costing instead of standard absorption costing, there will be two differences in the way variances are calculated.

1   In a standard marginal costing system, there will be no fixed overhead volume variance

2   Total sales margin variance ➡ Replaced by total sales contribution variance

3   Operating statement ➡ Absorption costing begins with budgeted profit

➡ Marginal costing begins with budgeted contribution

One way in which the examiner can test your understanding of variance analysis is to provide information about variances from which you have to 'work backwards' to determine the actual results. You need to take an algebraic approach.

The syllabus for Management Accounting Fundamentals states that you need to be able to prepare accounting entries for an integrated accounting system using standard costs.

STORES LEDGER CONTROL A/C

	£		£
Bank/creditors	X	WIP (actual quantity × std price)	X
		Material price variance (A)	X
	$\underline{X}$		$\underline{X}$

DIRECT WAGES CONTROL A/C

	£		£
Bank/creditors	X	WIP (actual hours × std rate)	X
Labour rate variance (F)	$\underline{X}$		
	$\underline{X}$		$\underline{X}$

17: Further variance analysis

PRODUCTION OVERHEAD CONTROL A/C

	£		£
Bank/creditors	X	WIP (actual units × std rate)	X
Volume variance (F)	X	Expenditure variance (A)	X
	X		X

WIP CONTROL A/C

	£		£
Stores a/c	X	Finished goods a/c	
Direct wages a/c	X	(actual output ×	
Production o/head	X	standard cost)	X
Labour efficiency		Material usage	
variance (F)	X	variance (A)	X
		Idle time variance	X
	X		X

The production overhead volume variance can be recorded in either the production overhead control a/c *or* in the WIP control a/c.

Sales variances do not appear in books of account. Sales are recorded in the sales account at actual invoiced value.

LABOUR RATE VARIANCE A/C

	£		£
Profit and loss a/c	X	Direct wages a/c	X

Notes

Notes

Notes

Notes

Notes

Notes